Women It's Time *to Take a* Bubble Bath

A True Story

Delisa A. Johnson

Delisa A. Johnson

Woman It's Time to Take a Bubble Bath

Published by Fountain of Life Publisher's House

P. O. Box 922612 Norcross, GA 30010
Phone: 404-936-3989
Please Email Manuscripts to: publish@pariceparker.biz
For all book orders including wholesale email: sales@pariceparker.biz
To request author email: author@pariceparker.biz
www.pariceparker.biz

Fountain of Life Publishing House is committed to excellence in the publishing industry. The Company reflects the philosophy established by the founder, based on Psalm 68:11, *"The Lord gave the word and great was the company of those who published it."*

Cover Design by Parice C Parker
Editor: Demetrice A. Benton

Published in the United States of America
ISBN: 978-0692708712
03.30.2016

Foreword

I am overjoyed by what God is doing in Apostle Delisa Johnson's life. I thank God for placing such a great seasoned prophetic Prayer Warrior in my life. Thanks, to a sister for helping to pray me through. God is using this great woman servant to do great damage to the kingdom of darkness. God has turned the tables on her enemy- the devil. God is using the bad and the ugly seasons of her life to shine a flood light on childhood verbal and physical abuse. God has caused Apostle to share many of the dark seasons of her life to provoke conversation, awareness, and emotional healing to many who have suffered at the hands of those who were supposed to shelter and love you. The Woman of God deals with the issues that Bi- Racial children must address. She was discriminated by her white family members before she could walk. The Woman of God shares how the odds were stacked against her, and the process of beating the odds. She takes you on an emotional, heartfelt journey. It is full of drama, self-discovery that uncovers generational sins, and curses. God has trained, and taught her how to deal with, and overcome the effects of being reared by unfit biological parents.

Jennifer Johnson, Author of Dream Killers

Preface

Bag Lady:

You DON'T WANT TO BE A BAG Person. Drop those bags, and allow this every day is relaxing moment to help you transform into the man or woman God has already preordained you to be. Drop anger, mistrust, suffering, pain, mental mistreatment, and childhood issues. These things have held you back from huge life promises, great purpose and destiny long enough. Come and enjoy popping the bubbles of disappointment, failure and become an eagle with eagle mentality, and the drive of an eagle. The sky is not the limit. God wants you to move into a holistic living and abundance of life. "God's Word Is Final." Cry, Scream, Pray and let it go because your destination awaits!

Delisa A. Johnson

TABLE OF CONTENTS

INTRODUCTION

Before entering into my mother's womb, God had a plan for my life. I was the promise, which God had already preordained with His purpose, and plan. Now, in this season is my destination. My child life was hard, full of knocks, and bumps, but I made it. I still endure storms, trials, and temptations, but that is a part of development. Some struggles were leading me to write this book which shows all things good, bad indifferent or self-inflicted indeed works out for the good. It states in Romans 8:28, All things work together for the good of those that Love the Lord and are called according to His purpose. "Women It's Time Out Take A Bubble Bath," shows how even though residue and era of judgment can cause pain as you toss, and turns in your life. God's Word and promises are going to be fulfilled. "Women It's Time Out Take A Bubble Bath," will show you how to shake generational curses, and familiar spirits. You will find yourself laughing and crying but you will also find it cleansing plus strength to pass all your pain. Our suffering is a way to reach the promises of God, purpose and destiny that's planned for you.

Delisa A. Johnson

"Women It's Time Out Take A Bubble Bath"

This is a book of transformation I dedicate this book to my Instructor in Chicago; Il'

Grab that Bubble
Chapter 1

"Women It's Time Out Take A Bubble Bath," is a tool to help those that have felt helpless, to turn their lives around with the guidance of the Holy Spirit. I will help guide you to a place of peace, and cause your joy to be restored. The enemy has taken so much from you. It's time you release the pain, guilt, and shame as your weapon to beat the enemy at his own game. He tries to use your issues of life to kill your spirit and destroy your self-worth. Let's began by running some water as a purifier, and the bubbles are your life issues. Some may feel this is a stupid and unnecessary but it symbolizes cleaning up. Most of us consider taking a bath as a place of peace, and tranquility and for others to get away. As a woman, you will be able to understand. Let's make our bath water. I love mines hot and put your favorite bubble bath or bath oil in the tub. You want this bath to be unique. Light several candles and incense make sure it's a fragrance you love. You can put on your favorite tune, and stretch out, then allow yourself to relax. Lay back, begin to flow with the peace and just relax.

Go back with me to the time when you began to recognize that you didn't feel good about yourself. Let us began by laying back AND Saying A Prayer. Your prayer should speak to your enter child that needs to know that God is getting ready to take you through this incredible transformation. We are always are learning, and growing, but we need to understand that some things stay with us. Men I will come back to you because you wouldn't enjoy the bubble bath series. However, women let us began with this prayer; Lord we need your help at this point to guide us into our wonderful transformation.

Step 1

God show me how to forgive others. So I can move from a dangerous place too healing.

Step 2

Teach me how to forgive me.

Step 3

Show me how I should love myself as you love me.

I should have a love for myself as He loves me. I can share His love for others as He showed me before I knew how to love myself. I used everyone else for the reason that I was never happy or incomplete. I remember the song by the greatest music genius the late great Michael Jackson. “I am looking at the man in the mirror; I am learning to change my ways," In other words I should change me, and let others work on their stuff. This is how you become a bag lady. You have your stuff then you pick up other peoples' stuff, and start carrying their issues, when yours is already plenty.

So right here we are going to bust the next bubble, the bubble of your garbage, and others. If you can get rid of your bags, and others stuff that you've been holding. Now, let's grab that bubble, and pop it. Free yourself. We can fix others but don't take the time for self. Lord help us to let go of our pass by forgiving ourselves, and others from past hurts, pains, and offensives. Lord we have been holding on and keeping us from reaching our true destination. Give us or restore to us the self-love, the love that can give us a peace of mind, the forgiveness that we need to move closer to You, and Your promise in the mighty name of Jesus hear this prayer. You said in your holy word, If I press toward the mark of the high calling in Christ Jesus forgetting those things that are behind me," and pressing toward the mark for you.

That's in you Christ Jesus. Now breathe, and pop that bubble. Allow yourself, this time, to cry out, and say, "Lord thank you for the freshness in you." Go ahead, and give him the glory because He is worthy of our praises. He has seen us through and brought us out. Now, take a deep breath. Let it out slowly, then taking in a deeper breath, and as you release this one say out loud, "It is over, and I give it to you Lord, It is finished." Well, are you starting to feel the relief? You can repeat any of these at any time you need to be revived; I still go back sometimes to refresh me. Let's move on.

Next bubble is a little harder. This is the part where we get into why we make some of the choices that we make. Some things we do are self-made from just trusting our understanding, but we should learn to trust in the Lord and lean not to our own understanding. In all our ways we are to find out how to acknowledge Him then He gives us a promise. He shall direct our path. Now the problem is we always think of ourselves by being selfish then when it's messed up we begin to blame others, and yes even God. I use to say to God, I can't speak for you, but I had the nerve to say to Him, God why you let me? I would hear the voice of the Lord say, "This was your choice, and I let you find out that it's not what I was showing you to do but I, love you enough to allow you to do it your way." Now, you have the nerve to ask me why?" Maybe I say to you why you didn't do it my way, and you wouldn't have to go through. "This means that you are so right, God. Who do I think I am asking and why? Then I repent and say "God what is it that you would have me to do?"

It's time for the next bubble bath, and by the way. How are you feeling now? When I first had to do this I felt drained, and that I surely should have made better choices. Now let's get back, and relax. Release your own mind, and reach for the mind of Christ. Let this mind that is in Christ Jesus being also in you. Take another deep breath and breathe in, and out! Get ready to let go of your stinking thinking. I borrowed that one from this pastor which she preached that until heaven received the news, Pastor Beverly Huff; unlike some people, I give credit where credit is due.

Let's get back to our bubble bath. Our thinking usually is the one thing that is the most difficult thing that we have to do. Bringing up all that stuff the thinks that will tear you down, and burn you out. How many of you will admit that you have problems with your stinking thinking? "I can truly admit it's got me in so much stuff that I could have avoided if I just allowed God to fix my mind. Let's get ready to pop that bubble of stinking thinking and rely on Christ to lead us, and guide you in His timing not our own. Now, it's time to grab that bubble and pop it. Say, "Lord I have allowed my thinking to take me places, and cause me to do things you didn't have planned for me but I am done. I put my mind and thoughts in your hand. So please pop it. It is finished." Now relax, and lay back take a deep breath and breathe in and let it out slowly. Release it, and it's gone.

We are now ready to go forward with people that have been a hindrance to us. We have allowed their actions, and reactions to take us out of character. Now, lay back this can be difficult because a lot of this can be generational curses that are inherited. Let's prepare to pop this bubble but before we do. We must call out the names of those that have caused us pain, bad character flaws, and bad attitudes. It's time to release them, and yourself. So you don't have to become a bag lady when I first was called that by my transformation instructor. I took it in the literal sense, but it is baggage. Things, stuff, bad characteristics, and attitudes, all of these things cause us to be bag ladies, and we carry it into relationships. Besides, we carry this mess into family lives, our children, and not conscious of the pain, distrust, and disappointments that trigger down. So, I say to you, "Loose those people, situations, and circumstances that became heavy baggage." You don't want anything or anyone to distract you away from your purpose and promises. God has everything waiting for you when you're ready to receive it. Now reach up, grab that bubble, and pop it. Say out loud, "No more holding on to pass hurts, pains, and character flaws, other people actions and reactions." No more generational curses! Now, ask God to replace what you release with His joy, peace, love, long-suffering, and the peace that passes all human understanding.

Now, pop that bubble, and breathe in deeply, and let it go slowly. Now, pray in your words that you are in full forgiveness, no matter if the person is here or gone and now release it. Don’t allow it ever to come back or even enter your thoughts again. Remember, forgiveness is not for others. It's for you, and it shall make you free. And who forgives is truly forgiven. Now, it is complete don’t allow yourself to bring it up ever again just let it go!

Let Go & Let God
Chapter Two

The bubble of forgiveness was the most difficult, but I remember clearly that I felt so much weight being lifted off of me. I never will pick those bags up again. I learned that God is not like a personal guard dog. He desires for all to enter in not just me. So I remembered vengeance is of the Lord's, not mine. I am going to do my part and let it go. Everyone has the same opportunity as me to let go and let God. I found myself beginning to pray for those that mistreated me. No more being a bag lady. Now, I am free and able to reach the purpose and the promises of Him who sent me.

Now, we have decided not to allow things that were our baggage is our God, but to allow God

Almighty to move us into our purpose. So we can *get to our promises.* Now, pop your bubbles of past disappointments, and use this to symbolize a fresh start. Here we go first childhood bubble disappointments, mistreatment, abuse, and bad things that caused low self-esteem. Get ready pop all those bubbles. God take these terrible things that have controlled my success and help me to reach my full purpose. I want to receive all my promises. Paul said it best in Philippians 3:14 New Living Translation, "I press on toward the goal to win the prize for which God has called me heavenward in Christ Jesus". Now pop those bubbles and move on to the greater you.

Now all the bubbles have been popped, and we must put the new concepts that will cause us to be more successful and make us proud. We want our Heavenly Father to be glorified. We are now ready and capable of being the best we are called to be. We are living examples that with God all things are possible. Scripture for this is also from Apostle Paul in Philippians 4:13 the New Living Version "For I can do everything through Christ, who gives me strength." It is now time to relax and began to say to yourself, I am special, and God has equipped me with everything I need. I can do all things that I have imagined and know it was God's will for my life. Now, set back, take a deep breath in and let it out very slowly. This time, let go and take another deep breath. Let it out slowly, and take in a positive energy that should be surrounding you. The Holy Spirit is cleansing you and that the best is yet to come. The Spirit of God can now lead you to your destination and promise because now can receive those things that God has already placed inside you. If you finally feel that release in your heart, you are now on your way. As you are waiting for that moment of receiving your promise, if the enemy brings up your pass or that old baggage, you, continue to remind him of your future. And ask God to give you more strength to be an overcomer. Satan is trying to take you back say to him, Romans 8:37 New Living Translation "No, despite all these things, overwhelming, victory is ours through Him who loved us." We have come to the end of our bubble bath. But we now can work on ourselves daily, and we can use the bubble bath anytime that it is needed. You can now look into your mirror of self-examination. Look and affirm yourself with knowing that God has started something within you, and He shall complete what He has started. Thank you so much for allowing me the privilege of being a guide in "Women It's Time Out To Take Bubble A Bath," one there is much more that shall come forth. Now, don't you think it's easier to take a bubble bath than worry about your past?

Who Is My Mother & Father Chapter Three

My Life

There are parts of my life story that I was told by relatives and friends that I decided to share with you. The majority is from my experience. Now, this is what I call a start. My life story begins with two young people that had a child when they were young and during terrible times. At this period, bi-racial children and bi-racial relationships were rejected by family plus society. My birth mother's family didn't except my birth father neither their bi-racial child. My birth mother use to tie my botties real tight around my ankles because they say, "you could tell I was a black baby." Her family would not keep me while she worked, and my biological father's family was just as bad. My birth parents seem to have no help. My grandparents on my father side would show up at my birth mothers job with me. It caused her problems the management and they would get angry because she dealt with blacks. So, from my understanding, she couldn't find a place for us to stay either. At this time, she asks my biological grandmother to allow me to stay with her until they got housing. So my grandmother agreed, and others did not want me, but I stayed.

They would put me in the large chair by the door. It was hot because there were only fans and no air conditioning. Every day they sat me in that chair and one day this woman came in. She asked, whose pretty baby is that?" She picked me up, and I was wet. It was a terribly hot and miserable day. My bottom was hurting from not being changed. She took me into the bathroom and washed me up. This lady told the man to buy some diaper rash and pampers. He did and a couple of sundresses plus sandals for my feet. My mother made me comfortable and held me then fed me. She also rocked me to sleep. About the time, she rocked me to sleep my grandmother said, "You know the little bastard is up for adoption." Neither James nor Betty wants her. So the woman said, "Brooks, I want her if she's up for adoption?" Brooks contacted his brother and asked, "Is this baby up for adoption?" James said, "He was about to being sent to jail, or the nut house and Betty can't keep that baby, so yes." The man, and woman packed up my things, took me with them to their home. Once I got there I must have felt comfortable, and the lady said, "I let out a relief and went to sleep." I slept the whole night, and they checked on me in the morning, and I still was asleep.

She said she tried to wake me to feed me, but I just went right back to sleep. Later on, in the evening, I woke up they fed me ate and went right back to sleep. They were concerned because I didn’t cry not even if I was wet? They said, "She was such a happy baby to have been through so much." James called and said, "Betty was crying and wanted her baby back." So they came to pick me up and took me with them. James called Brooks the very next day, and said, "if you want her I am bringing her to you because she is crying and won't stop." She wants to eat, and she doesn’t even want us to touch her. So bags and all he returned me to the Brooks and Dorothy. They adopted me, and we became a family. Now, you do understand that my father and mother, biological father is my adopted father's brother.

No! Mommy No!
Chapter Four

My story might get a little confusing, but you should have been me. My daddy and mother gave me a good up bringing for a while until things went sour quickly. They got a divorce, and I barely got to see them because of my mother She had issues with my daddy family. Slowly, but surely things went real sour very quickly. I, my mother, my aunts, and family were happy for a while. My Auntie Tee Tee loved me, and we spent lots of time together. My Auntie use to take me on her dates, bowling, movies, to dinner and whatever she did on the weekends. I was there. Another Aunt Dean Wiggins, Bibbs did my hair and gave me all my holiday parties. I was always my daddy beautiful little princess. I remember my first date was with my daddy. I was so excited he picked me up, and we went to the Black Curtain on Talbert.

My daddy showed me how a young man was supposed to treat a lady. On our father and daughter date, he opened the doors for me and pulled out my chair. He also showed me what to do with my dinner napkin on my lap and how to order. And, we even had a dinner drink before dinner. He had a real drink, but he ordered me a Shirley Temple. He taught me to sip and not drink it all down at once, and then we watched the show. During the show, they served salad before my first course. My daddy taught me my salad fork from my dinner fork, and then we had steak, baked potatoes, and ice cream for dessert. At least, I thought it was ice cream, but my daddy corrected me and told me it was chocolate mousse. We had a very good time. After that, I saw less of him, until I got up in some age. I thought for a long time maybe I am a bad daughter that's why he doesn't come around, but it was the issues with my mother that keep him away.

I found out later after years had passed that my mother had stopped working. She was home all the time, but she became bitter over time. Life was hard to deal with, and she began to drink like a fish. She became mean, and downright abusive. I went through so much at times. She would slap me across the room for no apparent reason or beat me because she was angry. Then, she would wake me up, and say she loved me. I sang while she played the piano, and I that would work for a little while then she would get sleepy and go to bed.

I was about five years old and was preparing to go off to school. I was excited about school, and it would give me a break from the craziness at home. When I first went off to school, I was so excited about it, but then the kids began to tease and pick on me because of the clothes I wore. Also, how my hair was done. One thing I can say. I didn't mine any of those things. I just wanted to be friends and play to get my home life off my mind. However, children can be cruel, and the teachers, well as the school representatives didn't help me. Every time I went to them, they called me a crybaby and a tattle tell. So I stop telling, and just allowed others to say and do whatever they wanted to me. I had a friend who was my doggy, and his name was Skippy. My dog made me happy and my dolls.

About that time in my life, I was going to the fourth grade, and I heard a voice. This one lady starts calling me in to speak with her. One day my teacher came over and touched my arm. I screamed bloody murder, and the next thing I knew I was in this lady's office. She was asking me questions then the police came, and ask me some more questions. I said nothing, so they called my mother, and told her they were bringing me home.

When we got there they made me undress, and they took some pictures. Also, they listen to what mother had to say and left. And no sooner did they leave; I got another beaten for them coming over to her house. She put in the basement and locked me down there. My best friend came with me, Skippy, and he let me lay on him. I cried, and he'd lick my face as I went to sleep. We laid down and slept, later my mother unlocked the door. She told me to go to bed without any supper, and I better not say anything else to anyone.

So when I got to school the next day that lady came to get me and ask me so more questions. I looked her in the face, and said, "Leave me alone you can't help me, and I am not saying anything else. Can I go back to my classroom please?" She said, "No, they want us to talk from now on." I said, "I am not saying anything else because you guys left me, and I got in more trouble. I have nothing else to say." So after about two weeks they stop letting me go there because I wouldn't talk.

I started doing things all by myself. I learned to entertain myself, so my time became about me, myself, and I. I didn't trust or like people anyway because I felt I was just there. Nobody ever noticed my pain or loneliness. So I learned just to be by myself unless I was with my cousins. Sometimes they didn't let me go. Most of the time, I was on punishment, for one thing, is another.

School went on and for some reason I had a hard time with math or arithmetic as they called it, I didn't like nor understand it and if I ask my mother she would explain it, but I just couldn't seem to pick it up. So of course, I got bad grades in it. And that meant I got punished. One night I was having trouble with my time's table and didn't do it right. My mother got so angry at me. She slapped me away from the table and grabbed me up got a rope, then hung me upside down in the door way. Don't ask me how? All I know is I was hanging by my feet upside down until I got the problems right. She gets me for so many things. My mother would beat me with wire hangers until I bleed, or cords that were thrown around, flower pots, chairs, or just hit me with her fist in my mouth, my head, my back, and my stomach. I didn't understand why she hated me so much? I got beat, so much I would fall out just to make her stop. But after the incidents she would make me bath water with salt, and make me wear long pants or long sleeve shirts so that no one could see the marks. I remember the marks they looked like worms with blood in them. If my face had marks, I'd say, "I fell while I was playing." I learned to lie and cover up real good.

I loved to sing, so I tried out for the school choir in sixth grade and got in. Singing was my get away from pain, being scared, and just relaxing. I felt the pain release when I song. It was excellent. I remember for my try outs, I sang Roberta Flack Killing me softly, and everyone applauded! Also, my father had now started seeing me more, so that was fun.

I remember I got furious when he first told me about his new wife. I thought he had betrayed me. I was his princess, how could he marry someone else, but he brought me to meet her I tried to play hard but my stepmother won me over she was kind an sweet and patient with me shed help me with my math and I began to get better grades and had a better understanding. She was cute and smart and nice, I liked her and began to love her and she made sure my daddy stayed in my life. As for that mother Bernice, I thank you.

It is about this time, the sixth grade class had a trip going too Washington DC, my mother said I didn't have enough money to go so I ask my father and stepmother to send it to me and they did. Pretty much anything I asked of them they would do it without hesitation. So I went to Washington DC, stayed in the hotel and got my very first crush on Lesley Winfro, he was cute, he had money or his family did. He brought me a gift while we were on the trip; we set together and talked for hours.

When we got back we were a couple or girlfriend and boyfriend we would ride our bikes together or just talk on the phone for hours. He was a nice young man. Then we broke up, he liked another girl and started seeing her and dropped me. But there was another young man that I grew up with in my neighborhood and we started talking and seeing each other up to my first year of high school. Then we fell apart but Bobby

Rogers was my actual first love, than we graduated from grade school he moved we lost touch.

I Had No Help

Chapter Five

In high school I began to open up a little more, don't think that things got better at home not by a long shot, but I'd really become numb with all the beatings. I just said to myself that I am going to do well in high school and get my own place and make myself happy. That's how I shut the pain out. In high school I still didn't have a lot of friends because I just wanted to get my lessons and go home. That was all I did up to my junior year, stayed to myself. I had worked so hard in school that I had all my credits and could either graduate early or stay and graduate with my class I decided to stay but all I had to do was come in sign the attendance book and leave so I went out and found me a job.

My mother wouldn't buy what I wanted or helped me, so I got my own job so that I could have what I desired. I went to Olan Mills photography studio and applied for position as a telephone sales person. I became good, within two weeks top sales within a month I was top sales person and was offered a new position as Telephone Sales Manager. I want you to know that I was making take home pay $900.00 a week without my commission. I could make as much as $1200.00 per week. However now I had a new problem. My very first pay I was so excited that I finally could have my own money, buy my own clothes and shoes. I started my own account and was excited to just have money in my pocket. But my dream was very short lived, my mother had other plans.

I knew my mother had used me to get money, she use to have me as her food deliver person in my younger years. My mother started selling dimmers to make extra money and promised to pay me; she'd give me $5.00 at the end of running around. It became a joke to the neighborhood that I was the cheeseburger girl. Might have been funny to them but it hurt me but I took it.

She sold Avon and I was the delivery person for that, she always had one thing or another to make extra money. So just to say in my young life I never had a childhood. My very first friend was chosen for me; my mother was outside working in her yard. She spoke to young lady, and ask her would she be my friend. The girl said okay let me meet her; we met and did truly became lifetime friends.

Rochelle Lee which I give thanks to for being a friend all through it. My mother pretty much dominated my entire life, everyone that was in life at a young age was chosen by her. She was a dominating force, she became my voice, my thoughts I was truly under her control; so I was excited to finally be independence of her and her ruling over my entire being so I thought, my mother had other plans. I got off from work took my check, got in the car with her she started right away with what I owed her. The list included gas money and rent; bills come before anything so she took it all but $20.00. What could I do with that? But just to have peace of mind I did it.

I continued to work and give my mother my money. She would spend my check as if I went to work to serve her needs, wants and desires. One week I came home and she said we going to move you're going to help me buy another house. We went to this house on 32nd Graceland Ave. When we got to the house and went in I was scared, the walls in the house where black with ABC's on it. The floors were wood and there was a master bedroom and a large den and another bedroom and a kitchen that was nice size a big backyard and an unfinished basement, and a half a bath and a full bath. She said we're going to redo this house of course, whatever makes you happy mother, so my next paychecks and all the other monies she had already taken, went toward the purchase of the house. She had already got a new car and then she brought paint and other things for us to redo the house.

For the next two months we would go after work and fix on this house. Once we painted and started cleaning it, I could see the potential. But I was under the impression that we were buying it for us not just her.

That is what she said, but I soon found out that everything belongs to Dorothy Gamble. Soon my mother was seeing a man name Donald Rogers and the next thing I knew he was my step father, poor man he just didn't know what we was getting his self into. But I was happy, maybe now she would let me keep my money. But, no way, she had to be in control of all things in everyone's life including my stepfather. He only got to keep $20.00 dollars from his pay I watched him become miserable and unhappy. It wasn't long before he started to drink and stayed drunk most of the time. He was under her ruler ship, that's how she did anyone that was in her life I brought her drinks and cigarettes and anything else she wanted just to keep her happy but nothing actually made her happy.

I continued to work pay her bills and give her whatever to keep her pleased. But as her drinking progressed, my mother's anger did also. She was always yelling and arguing with me and my stepfather for one thing or another.

I was about 18 years old and we found this dog that was cute ugly? about he had a bad habit of humping peoples leg and most people just reach down make the dog stop but not her one day myself and my step sister? where in the front room and she had been drinking all day and my step father too. The dog started humping my step father's leg and because he knew the dog he just sort of ignored it. He was feeling good from drinking and he just laughed and keeps talking. All of a sudden my mother came from out of the bedroom. She told my my stepfather that since he was not stopping the dog, that he must enjoy the dog humping him. She accused him of having a relationship with the dog; of course, we all laughed thinking she was just playing. It wasn't until we saw her face when said that the dog would have to go. She began to yell at the dog and tried to kick him, he ran and she grabbed the dog and kicked him out the gate. We thought maybe the dog would just sit but we watch the dog as he ran down the street and kept running. We never saw him again. My mother continued to accuse my stepfather about the dog until he said you are sick woman you need real help. She snapped and threw something at him he left and went outside to get away from her.

My mother had sexual issues; she was strange about being in any relationships. Later that day, my new friend came to pick me up. I was still in the bedroom getting ready, she started talking with him and he told me that he would be outside waiting for me. I finished getting ready and she came in and said you can't handle that man he needs a real woman. I just ignored her but once I got in the car with my friend John said "Honey, I am not being funny but your mother was hitting on me." I told John that she's crazy when she drinks so I thought nothing else about it. But it did stay in the back of my mind. When I came back off my date she would check my underwear and smell me to see if I smelt like sex, she would not allow me to take birth control. But the truth be told, I was not even interested in sex, I was more in to having a good time going out to eat or movies. I knew I couldn't have anything as long as I lived with her. She controlled everything.

I continued to work and was preparing for my graduation and prom. I had never really been shopping by myself and I was looking forward to buying and preparing myself for the graduation and prom. I wanted to do like all the other girls at school and a young lady that was an associate of mine. They were all talking about going shopping together for our things. So, I called and explained to my mother that I was going shopping she said as usual you should just come home. She said that we will go out and find my dresses and the other stuff together. I wanted to do it on my own so she said okay.

Finally I and the young lady went shopping together. I choose not to say the young ladies name because she has turned her life around now and become a preacher and we have seen each other. We went downtown to find our dresses and we started at JC Penny's and we walked in together but as usual, I had to check in at home. So I went straight to the pay phone to call my mother, which actually saved me this particular time. Because the young lady that was with me said that she couldn't find anything and wanted to go somewhere else.

As we were on our way out the door a man approached us and told us to come back into the store. We were then taken into a room and the door locked. She was in one room and I was in another. I had begun to get angry and asked why was I being detained and I had not done anything. The man stepped out of the room without answering me, and then he brought my associate into the room and opened her purse. In her purse were underwear, a pair of sun glasses and some perfume. When they then opened my purse I had nothing, but they said because we came in together, that they had to lock up both of us. She was crying and I was constantly threating her saying "I am going to kill you for putting me in this; my mother is going to kill me."

We got downtown and I was lucky that the security officer said this young lady came in and went straight to the phone. The other young lady walked around by herself and then walked up said something to this young lady and began to leave the store. My story matched everything that the security officer said so I was being let go. However, they still wanted to call our parents. When they called mine, I asked them to call my father instead of my mother and I gave the officer his name and number. I was lucky one of the officers knew my dad. They called and my daddy came but the officer said that he had called my mother also. He told me that she said that for my part I wouldn't be going to the graduation or the prom. My dad talked with her and explained that I didn't do anything but being with the wrong person.

When I got home I begged to please be allowed to attend my graduation even if I couldn't go to my prom. I was so proud that I had made it through high school especially with all that I had gone through to make it. My graduation day came and my daddy and my stepmother came but I was looking for my mother. Oh she showed up loud and drunk. She embarrassed and ashamed me by the way she acted. But I graduated and that was a great accomplishment to me.

We all left of course, I rode with my dad and stepmother, and my daddy said he was so proud of me. When we arrived to the house, my mother was still feeling no pain; she said she had gotten me something. It was a new stereo system, I was so excited but this didn't last long. I soon was told by her that I needed to make the payments and don't use unless I ask permission. My dad and stepmother where tired of me trying to get around so they brought me my own car. It was a 69 Dodge Palabra. I named her wild cherry; she was burgundy with a black top. I was so happy I could get to work and school.

I had decided to go to Aristotle College to be a dental assistant. I want you to understand that I did all these things to try and make my mother see that I was a good girl. Nothing worked though; I remember her words they rang in my ear time after time. "You will never be anything or have anything." So anytime I felt good about what I did I could hear just those words. I continued to work at Olin Mills Studio, until they closed down.

I was still in school but I soon got tired of school and trying to babysit my mother and all her issues. I was tired of not having my own money and by now it all had started to really take its toll on me. The one thing I realized is that I was never good enough know matter what I did.

One day I got on the bus, I rode it downtown to clear my head. As I was walking, I ran into a young woman that I had not seen in forever. She invited me to come to her place of employment and have a drink with her and I did. When we got there it was quiet and only the bartender, the boss, her daughter, my friend and I who were there. So we sat down and she had a strong drink and I had a cola because I just didn't like liquor. Then other girls started coming in and she asks me to excuse her. They all went down some stairs and then all of the sudden they came upstairs on the song, We Are Family; they got on stage and started dancing. The customers started clapping and cheering and then the gentleman started giving the girls money once they started taking off their clothes. When they were finishing dancing they came off stage and started sitting with different customers. This is how I was introduced to being a stripper.

I sat for a while than my friend came back to the table and she began to count her money. And it was a lot of ones, fives, and twenties. I soon found out how the job worked and then I ask how I could do it because I needed the money after the company closed. My friend asked her boss if I could try out. She gave me an outfit. I was so scared but yet I was excited, but once I got on stage I was nervous but what saved me was that I could dance. I started moving and the girls started throwing money and the DJ gave me my stage name, Honey. I liked it so I kept it. The men started giving me money. I was excited from the money and the attention. It made me feel important and that I was special it was something I felt that I missed out on at home. I danced and came off the stage with hundred and fifty dollars in one set. I found that's what your time on stage is called.

The boss asks me to go change my clothes then come back and speak with her. She offered me a position and I accepted with one exception, that I could only one work the day shift and she said okay.

I started that very day but I called and told my mother I got a job downtown and that I would still be able to pay my rent and bills. I would work from 11:00 a.m. to 7:00 p.m., you might think it was bad but I could make more in two sets than I could make on one job for a week and still enjoyed myself. However that changed because even though you made good, the boss found ways to tax the money. She charged a stage fee, a drink fee, yeah you have to be hustler, something I didn't know one thing about, but learned quickly. However I got my steady customers and I had them pay my stage fee and buy me fake drink. Yes, mine where fake because I didn't like liquor so I'd have the bartender fix me Virgin Long Island Ice Tea. My regulars soon started paying for my shoes and paid my bills, my rent, brought my mother gifts, diamond rings, fur coat, still nothing changed. I still didn't get love nor respected. I worked at the Clique for several years.

One day I heard about another bar called the Red Garter. I went in, tried out and got hired. It was a notch up from the Clique. They gave me a going away party but all day long I sort of felt funny. A while back I had ran into my ex-boyfriend from when I was going to church. We had been girlfriend, boyfriend without ever doing the do. Well this time when we got together things were different and the next thing I knew, I went to the doctor to find out I that I was pregnant.

I had to make a living so I continued to dance. The girls there sort of adopted my first born, my son while I was yet carrying him. They gave me a baby shower with so many gifts. Customers gave money and they even gave me encouragement. Eventually, I had to stop dancing but the customers and girls helped me so much, I was not in need of anything. And the Red Garter said for me to take my time, my job was in no danger. I had the most awesome baby doctor. If you still out there somewhere Dr. Conard, I just want to let you know that you are the greatest doctor. As I got closer to the time my son had started really making me big and tired, my blood pressure was high. I was so excited for my baby to come, I planned to be a great mother, love my child like I was never loved. I wanted to give him all that I could. My mother was even meaner as I started getting closer to delivery time. However her birthday was here so I wanted to give her a birthday like she had never had before.

Lord knows I tried; I made her favorite food, Lasagna and Garlic Bread. I brought her a beautiful cake, got her gifts and invited everyone over. Yes, I even brought drinks although she had already started drinking, but it was her day. We all were having a pretty nice time but like I said liquor and my mother just don't mix, it made her mean. She began to say stuff about that I was never going to be nothing not like her. She said her friends daughters' went to college, got nice cars and beautiful houses, husbands and children. She said, not my whore, she gets pregnant, no husband, nowhere to live except with me. She even said "Where I pay everything." not even remembering I was the one that helped her get her car, her house, her drinks and cigarettes. We were just about to finish up the party and she started in on me, all I said was alright mother just go ahead and go to bed I will clean up.

You would have thought I cussed her out, she jumped up grabbed a broom and said "I will knock that bastard baby right out of your stomach." Well that was about all I could take, she raised that broom at my stomach and something snapped I was ready to stop her from hitting me. I told her if she hit me with that broom I would defend myself and my unborn child. I was ready to hit her with the chair. We had words back and forth, my stepfather tried to calm the situation down but I guess it had finally come to a head.

I didn't hit her though; she's my mother I just got out. As I left, she threw a door rabbit at my head and it barely missed. I just kept on walking called my auntie; she and my uncle came and got me. I waited until my mother wasn't high anymore and returned home. It was getting closer to my delivery time and a little pass so Dr. Conard saw me and said you've held this baby long enough. He said that tonight is the last baseball game and he did not want me to interrupt his game. I said "Only God knows, Doc but okay."

I got back from my appointment and wanted pickles. I loved them old fashion dill pickles and chocolate ice cream. My stepfather said he'd go get me some, but my mother said her fat behind needs to walk so I strolled up to Mrs. Alexander's store on the corner. Once I got there I was so much out of breath she made me sit down before I walked back.

Just so happen, a friend that was driving came in and took me back to the house. Returning to the house I started feeling a tightening in my belly and I felt sort of up and energized. I laid down and woke feeling like I needed to go, and as soon as I stared toward the door I felt water running down my leg. I called out to my mother and stepfather who jumped up and got me to the hospital. They put me in a wheel chair and I guess they paged my doctor next thing I knew I was prep for going into labor.

I remember the nurse saying we going to have a baby, it seems like in seconds to me I heard Dr. Conard saying slide him on home girly. There he stood with the baseball uniform and his catcher's mitt he said "Didn't I say don't have this baby during my last game. Well here we go baby, everything looks good."

All of the sudden I could barely breath and I felt my heart rate slowing down then I barely heard them say the umbilical cord is wrapped and both heartbeats have started crashing. Dr. Conard went straight to work and both me and baby re-established. Then all the sudden I heard them say it's a boy, healthy and so handsome.

They rushed him over to something I couldn't actually see but then they brought him back and I saw the most handsome boy I had ever laid eyes on. They handed him to me and he was just chilling like so, who are you? I said "I am your mother and I have been waiting on you." Then I raised him up and ask God to take him back and I thanked him for allowing me to be the blessed one to have him. I woke later to the nurse bringing him for a feeding. He ate and my mother, stepfather, daddy and stepmother where all there. My Aunt Lee and Uncle Bill came to see me too. Everybody said the same thing, he is handsome. So right then and there I ask my daddy since I felt he was the most handsome man that I ever saw, could I name my son after him Jerdson Lamont Gamble. Jerdson is my daddy's first name. So, Master Jerdson was now in the house. I was so happy to have someone that I could love and someone to love me.

We both came home and I showed him my room and his bed. While I was yet bonding with my son, my mother started giving orders, "don't hold all the time and don't always get him when he cries, make sure you check his milk so you don't burn him." Now all these things she told me not to do she was doing every time I turned around she was doing something with are for him before me. She acted as if she was the mother and I was nothing. But I ignored all the signs because she was my mother and this was her first time being a grandmother.

You must understand through life with my mother I just wanted her to love me. Whatever it took I did, even when it made me feel bad about myself or I felt she was over stepping her bounds. She did everyone else like that as well, all but my Auntie Tee Tee, she would check my mother. My Auntie Tee, Tee was my savior when I was a younger. She would get me away from my living situation; sometime she'd pick me up and take me with her on her dates. She would let me have fun at her house. She dranked also, but she was fun, not an angry drinking person. While I was with her, she keep me feeling better about my problems. Then I'd have to go back but it was nice to get away for a while.

Back to me and my son I soon returned back to my job my mother keep my son and I had to pay her along with rent, utility bills, and she had even took a second mortgage that she had me paying for well. My stepfather didn't make as much as I did and my mother didn't have a job per say. She did sell Avon, ticket books and numbers. So in other words, I was the bread winner.

The Healing

Chapter Six

Just thinking back as I write this book, anger is trying to creep in, because all the ones that felt that I was such a bad child you should have been in my box and see if you feel the same. I will always say to someone else walk a week in my shoes and see if you wouldn't feel the way I feel. For so many years the boxes keep me from really feeling or really understanding my feelings. Thus arrives the name of my story, "living in a lock box without a key" not ever finding out until later that the key was within me.

I returned back to work dancing for the Red Garter and started making money so I decided it was time to strike out on my own. I started putting monies a side to get my own place for me and my son, as well as, buying things and putting them in storage. One of my regulars did real estate and found a cute house for me and my son in a quiet neighborhood. During the time that I was making all the preparations, saving up and storing my things my mother said nothing. The day that I was finally had everything packed up and about to leave, I got ready to pick up my son and walk out my mother turn into an even angrier person. I picked him up she told me to put him down, you can go but he's not going anywhere. She told me that I did not know what to do with him, his allergic to you he breaks out every time you touch him. I thought she was just playing so I kept on getting him together and all of the sudden she jumped up put a gun to my head. She told me that if I pick him up again that she would kill you or hurt me really bad. I was afraid she would hurt my baby so I left went and got the police. That did not do any good they told me that I would have to go to court. I did not know that my mother had already gotten a lawyer to stop me from removing my son. I cried but there was nothing I could do. I tried to get a lawyer but every time I said my mother's lawyer's name, everyone would back out. Her attorney was Max Ryerson. One day I was at the club and a man came in, he stood out because I never seen him in there. He ask me to sit with him and he handed me a card from Max Ryerson and ask me to come to the office the next day. I went to the office expecting to resolve me and my mother's issue with my son. Once I got there I was ask to have a seat and then Attorney Ryerson invited me into his office. He told me began with informing me that he was representing my mother and they had planned to show me as unfit mother. Then he pulled out an envelope that contained pictures of me dancing and taking off my clothes. He said that if I fought them that he would show the pictures in court. I was scared because he told me that we went to court that he would make sure that I wouldn't even be able to see him again.

I began to cry and when the court date came around I was there without a lawyer. I just simply said to the judge that I loved my son and wanted my son. All the evidence was stacked up against me. And to my surprise the judge was going to give my son to me. But Attorney Ryerson asked for a break. My mother walked up to me crying saying that if I took my son from her she would just die with a heart attack. She told me to just let him stay so she could help me with him. She said that he was so small and I would be working at night and sleeping during the day. She said she didn't want anyone else to take care of him and that I can see him and stay with him whenever I wanted.

Oh I forgot to say that my mother knew just how to manipulate me to get her way. I told you just to have her approval or love that she could get me to do anything. We walked back in the court room, and Attorney Ryerson said to the judge that my mother and I had made arrangements and that I had given my mother permission to allow her son to stay in her care. The judge asked me did I understand what was going on and I said "yes sir." He dismissed the case and said so it is as requested.

Now what I didn't know is that this meant that my mother now had guardianship over my son. I did not realize it until it was rubbed in my face by her when I went to see my son. She had got it all her way once again. The only time I could see my son is if I was bringing him money or presents, otherwise I was not allowed to see him.

I want you guys to understand that everyone was afraid of my mother. She was the kind of woman that everything was her way or no way. I would give my mother money, brought my son and her money for her bills to keep her happy. She was the kind of person that controlled you with what you would do to make her satisfied. I worked and paid her bills and brought her things and brought things for my son.

One day I got papers in the mail that she had gotten guardianship without me knowing because I was never notified of the court date. Since I didn't show up in court, she was awarded custody. I started crying and this time I found myself so upset I had a new attitude. I did any and everything I could do to hurt myself and her. I didn't understand I was only hurting myself. I became withdrawn from caring for anybody or anything. In the back of my mind I could hear her saying "you will never have anything or be anything" and I felt that way.

So I began to work and spend money like I'd lost my mind. I didn't care about what I did within reason. I had changed dance jobs from one bar to the next. In this I found my escape away from the pain. I started dancing at the Rafters until it closed. I had been in and out of relationships, staying at hotels and I was having sex to cover my hurt and pain. I was never a drinker or did drugs, as a matter of fact I loved dancing and was good at it. I had many friends that said to me constantly, "you just don't seem to fit in but you can dance."

As time went on I realized if I took my son away from what he knew it might hurt him. So I resided to the fact I wouldn't get him back but it didn't stop me from making sure he had what he needed and money. I thought my mother would tell him what I did for him but I found out later she took all the credit. She was even telling him that I just didn't want him which was not true. One thing I must state is that trying to keep her love, I lost myself and my so. At this moment I would like to say to my son "I don't blame you for not wanting to be in my life, if I could change what happened I would. But son, be assured of this, I loved you the best that I knew how. I am not using excuses just the bare facts, and in this time I ask for your forgiveness and pray that your life is all that you want." Please God protect him.

I started fading out of dancing and started working for Eddie at the Sun Set Strip. Lord while I was working here, I could tell so many stories. I became like a mother and big sister, helping several acquaintances with alcoholism and drug addictions that it became a passion. I had moved around from one place to another, but it was coming to an end.

One day I found out that my calling was catching up with me, I was upon stage and dancing to Purple Rain by Prince and all of the sudden I couldn't hear the music nor could I hear the people. In the midst of the dance I heard a clear voice say "choose you this day whether to serve man or me. I looked and on the side of stage was a black horse and upon the horse was dark shadow. This shadow was holding a sword of sorts like

I have never seen a sword. It was rounded and on each side and there were knives that stuck out in a circular figure that could cut my head off any way I would run. At the same time I saw a bright light and I felt within myself that I should run and I ran off the stage and up the stairs. I put on my jeans and a top, and a pair of boots. I grabbed fifty dollars and threw all my dance clothes and all the money in the streets plus gold rings, shoes and boots. I walked straight to the greyhound bus terminal, jumped in line and something say catch the bus going to Chicago.

Understand never had been in Chicago other than to visit my aunt and I remembered that I went there on an out of town trip with my sixth grade class. But we only looked at sites, we didn't know anyone there.

Before all of this I must back it up just a little, I did get pregnant again and had a beautiful baby girl. My mother kept her too but it was me this time that made the suggestion because I wanted my children to protect each other and know each other. However, it didn't work out well because my mother started in on my daughter. My baby girl was different than me and only took so much then she called the police on my mother. So my mother said she had to go. But my mind was still crazy at this time but I brought my daughter home to stay with me. I had moved out of the hotels by this time and had my own place. But I really couldn't be a good mother but I did try. If I could turn back the hands of time, I wished to the Lord I had done things differently. To my precious daughter I would like to say: "Thank you for your forgiveness. I know I took you through so much but I love you and appreciate that you have stuck with your mother through everything. I remember daughter that you would place your little hands on me when things were at their darkest place and say mommy it's going to be alright. I am sorry mommy trusted someone else to take care of you but I pray that you would be a better mother." And my prayers were answered and I am glad that I got another chance.

When I got my first apartment for my daughter and myself I thought the craziness was over. I worked and spent time with my daughter. There was another single mom across the hall from me and I won't state her name because I loved her and her children. I feed and clothed them and they were at my house a lot with Jessica my daughter and they adored her. But as I said before, I had a lot of things that I needed to learn. If I had to title this part of this book it would be lessons learned and burned.

This woman secretly hated the fact that her children where close to me so she arranged for me to be hurt by her brother. He came and knocked on my door and told me that his sister had sent him over to borrow some sugar. I thought nothing of it, it was not unusual for us to share. He came in and I went into the kitchen to get the sugar. While I was in the kitchen, he locked and bolted my door quietly. He came into the kitchen and stuck a pistol in my face and pushed me into my bedroom where he told me too undress and don't make a sound. He said that he would kill this sweet baby. When it was my babies in danger, I complied. This man stayed there for more than three hours and finally he got up ran out the door leaving it opens. I began to scream and crawled out and ask people to call the police.

No, they never arrested him or prosecuted him. But, fate brought him back to me one more time. He wondered into where I was dancing, I said nothing. I went right downstairs got my pistol and when I came back up and I starting shooting. Everyone was running and getting under tables but I kept shooting at him. He was running down the street. I didn't stop until the police came. Once again he was not caught and the police took me back to the bar. I paid my boss for all the damages and apologized to the customers and girls. I went home and grabbed my baby and held her. I began making arrangements for us to move.

I moved away from that apartment and changed jobs as well. I started working at the Sunset Strip, were I started not only dancing but worked on being a show girl dancer. I traveled different places, man I can tell you that you may think that you have plans on doing one thing and watch God change them.

I danced for about another two half years and left there and went to the Circus Club. The boss there saw more in me and gave me the manager's position until I quit my job. In between time I met a man and thought that I would give a relationship a try again. But man, I should have left well enough alone. I met a guy named Hakim, and we started seeing each other. When you say from the skillet into the deep fryer, this man was crazy and dangerous. This man was a player and a nut put together. Hakim found out that I was the manager of the Circus Club and he was planning to rob it. He was going to rob the bar, beat me up then, share the monies with me. I may have not been the best person in the world but this I couldn't do. So I told my boss and resigned. This man found out that I had messed up his plans and he tried to kill me. He acted as if everything was okay and took me to his apartment. He beat me until I passed out then he got me up the next day and dropped me off at my car. I was bruised up and very soar. I tried to act as if I was ok and I went to work to set up to open. The bar started filling up and the girls came in. By that time I began to feel really dizzy but continued to work. My step sister who worked there also came in and all of the sudden she screamed and ran and got the security. They ran behind the bar, grabbed me and sat me down. My step sister kept pointing at me and the next thing I knew, I was at the hospital. My face had swelled up and I blacked out. I woke up with doctors saying she could lose her sight, and her face may never recover. But I serve a God that didn't allow that. My face went back to normal.

When I got out of the hospital, I first went to stay with my stepsister because come too find out this guy had a lot of alias. The police could not find him. But he had let everyone know that knew me that he intended to kill me whenever he saw me. He'd been to my house with a gun and shot it up. I felt it was best for my daughter stay with friends and I get out of town. I left and moved to Georgia and then left there and went back to Chicago, IL. So many things had happened but I came back too Indiana once I was convinced that he was no threat anymore. I went back to the Sun Set Strip where I had the meeting with God and my choices. Where I was asked the question choose you who you will serve man or God.

I choose God ended up in Chicago, from there to Richmond Indiana in ministry a called Last Call for God's Love. There I fell in love with Phillip Johnson and he asked me to marry him. Then we went and got my daughter and moved to Atlanta. I thought life was going to be really good until I discovered a drug called crack. This drug can kill and tear everything down that you work hard for. It will just take it, I lost my car to drug dealers, lost money and my home. But to God be the glory that I had strong mother and father in law that I could count on.

I and my husband, and Jessica all went back to Chicago to live with them but to no avail crack followed us and things got worse. My husband became ill and he became hard to deal with so I left when I just couldn't take any more. I came back to Indianapolis, Indiana until my husband came to live with us again.

Things where fine for a while, understand I had a beautiful life with my husband when drugs were not a part of our life and some other things I can't reveal. But I loved my husband and didn't divorce him. When he finally got it together we were just getting ready to work our marriage out, I received a call that said he was gone. This was not a surprise to me for I remember making a statement to my husband that God had told me I wouldn't return until the conclusion of this matter. But I am sure of one thing, my husband did love me. There was just so much in the way, but God allowed me to hear for myself that he was at peace with himself. And God, called him back to his first love and he was excited to start new. God had plans for him and I shall always remember my first true love Phillip Johnson.

Now about the time God had really got me at a point in my life where I was ready to work hard in ministry. We finally got our outreach off the ground in Chicago, Ill. With the help of my mother and father-in-law, we worked tirelessly to put it together. It was a project that my husband had so much input in and we wanted continue his work. I chose to stay with my mother-in-law and work with her. We became Ruth and Naomi's story in real life. I ran both the women's and men's house with the guidance of both my bishops and God leading us all.

The outreach became so awesome, we were feeding the Southside of Chicago and also we had two singing groups. We had a male course which was awesome and also a choir that was great. We also gave out clothing and also feed the hungry during breakfast, lunch, and dinner. And all our people, young and old were attending church. We were growing by leaps and bounds.

God used the extended family to help so many, we all had love for one another. At first it was a hard getting the church off the ground, but everyone soon came around and found it was an awesome time. Some went on and did greater things; some went back to the streets. But one thing I will say is they never went so far they didn't know how to come back. Some came back for whatever their needs were. Some came back because they couldn't make up their minds to be in or out but we loved on them just the same. God thank you for the opportunity to see real love in action, sorry that I got caught in self and left my first love. The one thing I recognized out of this lesson is never let anything separate me from God. God never leaves us, we leave him and get caught up and then we realize we need our first love.

Quickly by this time I'd lost my faith and my way, trying to satisfy my own self-interest. But God never allowed me to go so far that I didn't know how to get back to my first love. I just want to take the time right here to say "Thank you God, I really thank you for your unconditional love."

About this time the outreach houses had closed but the outreach and youth choir was still going strong. I thank you Lord for allowing me the opportunity to work with the young people. They stirred my soul. I felt that they taught me more than I could ever teach them. I thank you Holy Angels Youth Choir and young people, you truly blessed me to teach, and see you grow up and be so awesome. You are still working and striving to become all that God has for you. Just know that I love you all. To all the ones that worked with me at Holy Angels Baptist church, my bishop for staying on me about my mouth. For my other bishops, who gave me the wisdom of not allowing me to be caught without someone who will always be there? To Bishop Jack Johnson & Bishop Mildred Johnson thank you for your love, understanding, guidance and for believing in the visions that God has given us all. I also want to thank you for your wisdom and awesome teaching which helps me to this day. I now understand the do's and don'ts and know I have a zeal and knowledge and how to love and not get caught up. You have been there for me as if I were your own not just a daughter-in-law. For all of this I thank you.

Soon I decided it was time for me to return back to Indianapolis and I tried so hard to fight going back into ministry. I wanted a time out but everywhere I went I'd get called out. You can't hide or take a vacation from working in ministry it will find you where ever you go. I returned back to Indianapolis, Indiana I went and worked with several different ministries. Working in ministry there were many obstacles that had to overcome. But when you have been chosen everything that you go through is a part of learning how to lean and depend strictly on God. He allows you to sometimes bump your head from disobedience. Sometimes you may go through for you to be a lesson or blessing for others. One thing I truly understand nothing that I've been through has come to make me stronger as well as be able to be a living testimony of God's word. So many times I found that my greatest temptation was man and myself. I always thought that everything and everybody should reach my expectations. But never did I give the same, there where many times it was for my own use or plan. I begin to see in myself being a manipulator and was good at it.

One day things switched on me and I met up with a greater manipulator than I could ever be. And the enemy knew my weakness laid in men or relationships. I always wanted to be the perfect wife and nothing was going to stop me from having. So you might say I came to find out that my greatest enemy was myself. I had not yet learned how to love or care about myself yet. I was preaching love, caring, and being honest but I was lying to myself and others that I was happy and complete.

Love was missing and in its place were distrust, pain and fake love, more like neediness'. One thing I can say as God had told me, I loved others but most of the time I felt it was really my weakness. In this God showed me that loving myself was all I needed to do, then others could love me. I was now able to tell the difference in real love and just lust use to get them mixed up.

During my ministry years traveling I gained vast knowledge of people as while as well as self-awareness. When I lost my first husband I decided to get in a program in Chicago that was called a transformation. It taught me how to prepare and get ready for job interviews. I also learned how to look at those invisible demons. I was blessed to have an instructor that saw all of my potentials and the work that God had with in me. But see also she saw the demons that I tried to cover by working hard and over achieve.

I thought I had done well in class, my last test I passed with flying colors both oral and written. I even did an awesome job on our group project. But that day we were supposed to get our certificates my instructor pulled me to the side and said I was a bag lady and she couldn't in good conscious allow me to graduate. She told me to go home and think about it. I was so angry that she was complaining about my bags I carried around which was my briefcase, my lunch and other things that I needed. What did that have to do with all that I contributed in my class? Even the other students didn't get it because I was everyone's mentor. So how was it I wasn't going to graduate? But as I got home and came to myself God spoke and said uzzziah must die. So I read the word and I began to understand that she didn't mean the natural bags, she was speaking that I had not release my baggage working on everybody else stuff I didn't take care of mine. I began to write on paper about myself. I began to see all my issues and allowed myself to heal with praying and seeing it written out on paper.

The very next morning I got in early and met with my instructor. She allowed me to graduate and told me that the spirit of Lord let her know that I was going to teach this transformation class. She had to be sure I had the concept of letting it go and allowing God.

Now the Lord is allowing me to write books for both men and women on transformation. So many times from this day to now God has allowed me to help others that or broken and feel defeated. Sometimes I tell him Lord this is a lot and he reminds me that to whom much is given much is required. The lord has used so much of my life to show me that I thought the key was outside the box but the Lord showed me that the key to leaving the box was inside me all the time.

During my time of transforming from what everyone else thought of me I found that God was there all the time and was waiting for me to recognize it was always within me. Now God is allowing me to grow and become his mouth piece and encouragement to those that are hurt and lost finding their way out of their box. All I can say is God is the glory I am free and willing to help those that can't find their keys. Thank you lord for all that I've been through and all that I still must yet walk through but I know that you are with me even until the end of my time.

DEDICATION

This book is dedicated to all that helped me to discover that tragedy in your life is God way it's leading you into the purpose and promise that God predestination before you even entering into my mother's womb.

BIOGRAPHY

Apostle, Prophetess, Delisa Ann Johnson

Being a child of The Lord and being groomed as a small young woman that was comfortable around the house of God. I stayed up under my adopted grandparents Pastor Felix Barnes and Glenda Barnes, God gave them to me in my life to groom me and teach me the word of God. In the house of

God I hung on too my grandfather his words and his integrity and Jesus character, he took me under his wing. Even though my home life was a struggle God shielded and allowed me to be protected and loved with real love. I would hang on to my grandfather's preaching and teaching. Even when we got out of service we'd go to their house, my grandmother was a piano teacher with anointed vocals. She began to teach me the piano but she soon found out I was the singer and a preacher. After hanging out with her I would go up to their bedroom and stand in front of the mirror and mimic my grandfather in totality of his sermon. I would then begin to shout and the Spirit would fall on me. Then I would become fearful but my granddaddy would come up smile and say "girl when God release you to your destiny you will show His glory." Later on in my first time of preaching my grandfather and grandmother was already gone to glory but I felt their presence. And I remember that afterwards I said God I hope that You and my grandparents are pleased. Growing up in my teen age years I fell more than I even would like to admit. There was so much wasted time, but God. I am almost ready to shout about how He loved me even when I found myself not loving me. At the pivotal point in my life I was a stripper in a famous dance bar in Indianapolis, Indiana making money had an automobile, clothes and jewelry but inside I felt empty an lost in self-destruction. But I remember early on God's plan, promise, and my purpose never changes. God word is final. On this point I felt I had it going on but I was standing on stage music blasting men yelling throwing money an also I was doing a dance to "Purple Rain" an all of the sudden in the midst of my dance I looked out of the corner of my eye I saw a dark shadow on a black horse. It had a sword that all sides had a blade that could cut my head clean off my body and in the midst of all the noise I heard a Loud Voice say, "Chose this day whom you shall serve God or man", It cause me to run up the stairs change my clothing throw all the money up in the air and jewelry an kept $150.00 dollars and was lead downtown too the Greyhound Bus Station. I looked up God said get on the bus headed too Chicago, Il. He had me get on the L train and ride it the train rolled me around for three days until this young woman got on a said I have seen you riding this train and I know you don't have a place to go do you. She said please get off the train and go with me to my grandmothers. I will be going to a program called "Last Call For God Love" and you can go with me maybe they can help you. We went to her grandmother's house and she received me and said she loved me as if I was her own. That Friday morning we got up and went and met the people in the program. At first I was fearful but God gave me a calm and peacefully spirit. And the pastor came through he told some they would be in the city program and others will be going to the country. They began to place us in our prospective places and before I knew me and the baby girl where placed on the van headed to our destination. I looked up and we were in Richmond, Indiana in the boonies. We pulled up and they asked us to get off the van. The pastor pulled up in his car playing, "Wake up Everybody." He jumped up and lined up all the woman and told them go on and put their stuff into the house he touched every one of them but me. When he came to me he walked on pass and then all he took me to the side and said what do you want from here. I said that God sent me here. He left me standing there and went inside the house and returned back with a woman and she got in his car. He then walked up to me and said woman of God go in and run the house of women. I was made right then and there the overseer of the house of women. So remember, "God Word is Final." To God be all the glory, I know that I was not worthy or even ready but God Word Is Final. Lord Thank You.

Apostle, Prophetess Delisa Ann Johnson

Bring about a mentally disturbed adoptive mother who made her life a living hell, and demolished her self-esteem, and self-worth, which open the door to self-hatred, and unhealthy life style, and a loss of zeal for living. But, through this entire ordeal God was making her into a mighty spiritual warrior. God has healed her and transformed her life. Now, God has assigned her to teach you and help the reader to wholeness, and transformation. So, I encourage you to place a yes, Lord in your spirit, and take out a pen and paper, as you read and begin the journey of Transformation.

Contact the Author and to Order more books:

Website: www.pushpastyourpain.org

Email: delisajohnson167@yahoo.com

Fountain of Life Publishers House

P. O. Box 922612, Norcross, GA 30010
Phone: 404.936.3989

For book orders or wholesale distribution
Website: www.pariceparker.biz

Woman It's Time to take a bubble bath.

www.ingramcontent.com/pod-product-compliance
Lightning Source LLC
Chambersburg PA
CBHW071744090426
42738CB00011B/2558